The Secrets of the Animals

Book 1:

Inside Your Amazing Neighborhood

Sandra Mendelson

© 2018 Sandra Mendelson

ISBN: 978-0-9992704-2-4

All rights reserved. This book may not be reproduced in whole or in part without written permission from the publisher. Nor may any part of this book be reproduced, stored in a retrieval system or transmitted in any form or by any means, electronic, mechanical, photocopying, recording or other, without written permission from the publisher.

Book Design by Deana Riddle

Cover Photo by Ben Winkler Photography

Interior Photos of Mister T provided by Vasi Studio and Ben Winkler Photography

Published in the United States of America

Discover the secret Animal Wisdom Ways so you can talk with the animals!

Join real-life dog Mister T on this incredible 3-part journey:

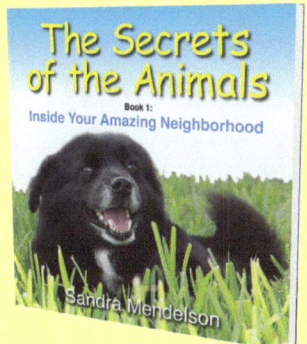

The Secrets of the Animals: Book 1
Inside Your Amazing Neighborhood

Discover the secret lives of the animals you pass by every day — and what they really want you to know!

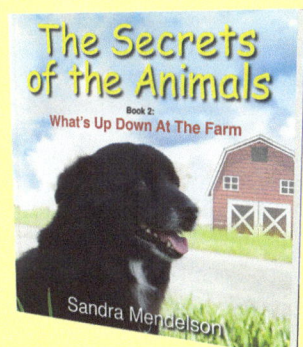

The Secrets of the Animals: Book 2
What's Up Down At The Farm

Large and small, feathered and furry, the residents of this farm reveal mysteries only animals know but you will find out!

Coming Soon!

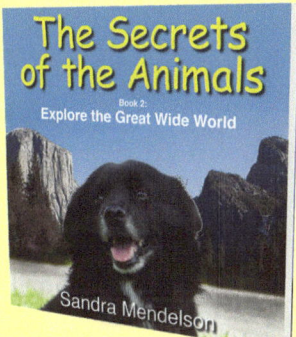

The Secrets of the Animals: Book 3
Explore The Great Wide World

In jungles, forests, oceans, deserts and plains the wildest of creatures await you with secrets they've kept since the beginning of time!

Coming Soon!

Please contact Sandra at smendelson.com to receive priority notification of upcoming book releases.

What makes this story special is that it's completely true

All animals communicate and they want to talk with you

It's a different kind of listening though, that you will have to do

Because your ears can't hear just where their messages come through

You may feel them in your belly or that space you call your heart

Or just have a sense of knowing – now that's a place to start!

If you're not sure which way to go to feel this stuff inside

Don't worry, you'll meet Mister T and he will be your guide

You'll learn the animals' secrets and you'll see it's lots of fun

When you at last discover you can talk with anyone!

Introduction

Mister T

Please let me introduce myself. My name is Mister T.
Did you know you were born with a special power so you can tell what animals are thinking and what we are trying to say? And boy, do we have a lot to say! The funny thing is, we don't talk the same way humans do, so to understand us you will need to use different parts of yourself. The animals will show you how!

Follow me now as we visit with some of the amazing animals that live right in your neighborhood. They will share with you some special secrets. We call them the "animal wisdom ways" and they are just waiting for you to come and find them. Are you ready?

Well let's go!

Mister T

To start on this journey you'll take your first step
When you catch ahold of the best secret yet
And this is the one you can practice each day
So you're starting to do things the animals' way
Is it hard? No! It's easy, and we think it's fun
So get ready, get set – here comes Secret One!

Secret Number 1: Remember You Are Love

Mister T

Put your hand on your heart, right there in your chest
It's the place all the animals love the best
For that's where you keep all the love that you are
And it shines from inside of you, bright like a star
This love that you are is a strong light that glows
From the top of your head to the tips of your toes
See yourself spread it all over the place
Send some to you too – to your body and face
And when you see an animal let your love flow
Because they love you back, wherever you go

How do you feel love inside of you?

Mister T

So where do we go to find Secret Two?

Let's ask the animals what we should do!

Well, here comes a seagull to give us direction

With a super idea that's just pure perfection!

Seagull

Start with the animals closest to you

Because they know you best and see all that you do

They may live in your house – are they dogs, are they cats?

Are they covered with scales, or feathers perhaps?

One cat in particular carries a clue

Come closer and she'll give you Secret Number Two

Secret Number 2: Notice Everything Around You

Cat

Just like a pencil, you can sharpen your sight
So like me you'll see more in the day and at night
Pretend you're a spy and your job is to see
What others may miss, you will spot easily
And along with your eyes you have other tools too
Like your ears that can hear when a bird sings to you
In fact, your whole body can sense things as well
And what others are feeling, you'll be able to tell
If they're nervous or tired, happy or sad
Or worried or frightened, angry or glad
You'll know so much more like the animals do
When you notice the littlest things around you

What little things do you see around you?

Mister T

While some other creatures may live in your house
Like hamsters and gerbils, a pet rat or a mouse
You must open your door and be ready to roam
To meet my wild friends in their natural home
Your next secret's waiting so come follow me!
Let's go meet the squirrel who holds Secret Three

Secret #3: Animals Can Hear What You're Thinking

Squirrel

Did you know that animals know what you're thinking?
It's like we see inside you without even blinking
We also can feel and can sense what is true
And the birds, they see stuff and they tell us too
So whenever you think of the things you can do
To be just the kindest and friendliest you
Remember the animals both near and far
Can hear all your thoughts and know just who you are
We choose where we go and the things that we do
So don't be surprised if we hang around you!

What thought do you want to share?

Mister T

Birds share the news from their place in the sky

As they can see everything from way up high

Which one brings a message you haven't heard before?

I believe it's a pigeon with Secret Number Four!

Secret #4: Animals Feel The Same Things You Do

Pigeon

We animals feel the same things you do
We all love and play and yes, we have kids too
If our feelings or bodies get hurt it feels bad
And when humans are mean it makes all of us sad
Our faces look calm and our tears do not show
But we cry deep inside, this you really must know
So we hope you'll be gentle and spend time with us
And see for yourselves we're not all serious
We are smart and we're funny and like all of you
We each have our own personalities too!
You'll see just how cool we are – just take a chance!
There's more to our lives than you'll see at first glance

What do birds say to you?

Mister T

Did you know some animals walk, fly and swim?
They're so busy moving they don't need a gym!
These talented folks include both swans and ducks
I see one ahead, looks like we'll be in luck!
She's headed our way as she swims and she glides
So say 'Hello Swan, may I have Secret Five?'

Secret #5 See Beauty Everywhere, Like Animals Do

Swan

This Earth is the home of such beautiful things
Like sunsets and flowers and dragonfly wings
And rocks that are shiny, and bees that go buzz
And neat caterpillars all covered in fuzz
A glistening web that a spider has made
Or perfect white eggs that a chicken just laid
Take a walk with your friends and you may be surprised
That you see different things since you each have two eyes
Show your friends what you see and have them show you too
So you'll see all the beauty the world holds for you

What beautiful things do you notice?

Mister T

Some animals hardly come out in the day
But when you're asleep, that's the time that they play
They're not scared of shadows or what's hard to see
Or monsters that really are just make believe
If you've got the spookies, this guy's got the fix
Come check out the bat who brings you Secret Six

Secret #6 Fear Is Mostly Made Up

Bat

When you see my face does it give you a fright?
Do you tremble when you hear some noises at night?
Does the thought of a scary dream fill you with dread?
Do you wonder if goblins hide under your bed?
You humans all fear things that live in your minds
But if you look around, you will see all is fine!
So when you have an icky thought stuck in your head
Take my advice and try this trick instead
Tell your family or friends what your fear's all about
Say 'Let's go for a walk, I must really get out!'
And you'll notice the awful stuff just melts away
When you breathe and say loudly 'I'm really OK!'

How do you stop being afraid?

Mister T

My dear friend the mouse knows more than you think
And she gets a lot done without making a stink
She brought along someone we'd both like to mention
He's a super great teacher – so please pay attention
Believe it or not, he's a chipmunk named Evan
Listen closely and he'll tell you Secret Number Seven

Secret #7 Say and Do What You Really Mean

Chipmunk

You ask why it is that I have a name?
Once I heard it and liked it and mine it became!
But I'm here to talk of a bigger concern
Something animals know but you humans must learn
You see that in our world we never tell lies
And fighting is rare and I'm telling you why
We say what we mean and the things that we do
Show the world who we are, that we're honest and true
Hear me now if you want to be friends we can trust
You must follow our lead – in this way be like us!

How do others know that you mean what you say?

Mister T

We know that this world can be one noisy place
When really loud sounds seem to fill every space
But animals know there's a time to be still
To turn down the volume and kick back and chill
So here comes an expert you should imitate
Come meet the wise rabbit who holds Secret Eight

Secret #8 Take Time To Be Quiet With Us

Rabbit

I'm a fast moving gal when I'm hopping around
But I live my whole life making hardly a sound
When machines are turned off and your ears finally rest
Then your animal skills can be put to the test
For we will come nearer and then you can see
Who we really are if you watch carefully
Take a break from computers and cell phones and such
And watch us in nature where you'll learn so much!

What does quiet feel like to you?

Mister T

You're truly amazing! You're awesome! You're great!

You've gotten so far that you've passed Secret Eight!

If you practice these ways you will soon have the knack

And there's still more to come so it's time for a nap!

Our adventure continues so don't be alarmed

We will meet once again to go visit a farm!

www.ingramcontent.com/pod-product-compliance
Lightning Source LLC
Chambersburg PA
CBHW041435010526
44118CB00002B/82